Beyond Putting the Toilet Seat Down

◆

423 Real Comments From Men and Women
About Their Relationships

◆

Written, compiled and illustrated by
Jack York and Brian Krueger

The Armchair Press, Cincinnati, Ohio

Published in Cincinnati, Ohio by The Armchair Press, 3616 White Oak Drive, Suite 2, Cincinnati, Ohio 45247.

For book trade ordering contact Publishers Distribution Service, 6893 Sullivan Road, Grawn, Michigan 49637, 1-800-345-0096 or call Ingram Books at 1-800-937-8000.

Printed by Eerdmans Printing Co., Grand Rapids, Michigan

Library of Congress Catalog Card Number 92-74490
ISBN 0-9634739-0-5

Printed in the United States of America

Introduction

The idea for this book came to us during a conversation with some friends over dinner one evening. One of the newly married couples said something to us that really opened our eyes. They said the key to a good relationship was not finding someone without faults, but rather someone whose faults you could live with. The couple probably didn't realize the can of worms they opened by making this statement.

What followed was an onslaught of comments, criticisms, gripes, likes, dislikes and everything in between. It turned out to be one of the most fun and entertaining evenings we've ever had. We went home wanting to hear more. We decided to write a book on this topic and wanted to talk to as many people as we could.

We developed a questionnaire and distributed over 2000 of them around the country. In addition, we conducted countless interviews with friends, family and pretty much anyone who would talk to us. We received over 3500 comments on topics ranging from bathroom habits to romance. We have chosen 423 of these quotes to share with you in this book. Because we consider ourselves armchair experts, you won't find a lot of psychobabble here - just real comments from real people like you. We hope you enjoy reading them as much as we did.

Brian Krueger
Jack York

Acknowledgements

OUR SINCERE THANKS to all who contributed to this collection of observations and insights: Kimberly Holiday, Linda Kain, Colleen Heyl, Amy Vonderbrink, Ken J. Bushman, Katherine Cox, Christina Stephens, Cindy Findley, Franci Thomas, Cyd Abner, Gina Bushman, Cara Miller, Chrissy Burns, Lee Ann Haering, Rachel Miller, Casie L. Vianello, Amy Cyrus, Rick Todd, Anthony C. Ewing, Julie Floss, Craig Clarke, Karen Chaffins, Chris Gliebe, Sarah Ott, Noelle Keller, Paul Krueger, Mary Kay Gerst, John E. Brooks, Dale Baumann, C. Peterson, J. Crawford, Sally Kline, Heather Gaynor, W.J. Yungbluth Jr., Art Sleeman, Hub Martini, Barb Michel, Chris Eglian, Bonnie Mackie, Alva Bettis, Linda Pelley, Sue Smith, Jenny Ferree, Victoria Adank, Nickie Gerdes, Cathy Cutter, Lauren K. Leitner, June Lindle, Bob and Eleanor, Glenn Estell, Brian Ainslie, Ken Cox, Christy Cox, Clifford York, Martha York, Jackie Evers, Ed Evers, Jeff Hoelker, Caren Hoelker, Kelly Brewer, Cass Brewer, Jenny York, Shawn McBrien, Kathy Zeinner, Andy Hauck, Suzanne Hauck, Carol York, Michael Dailey, Laura Dailey, Joe Hoelker, Louise Hoelker, Scott Murrer, Jennifer Sylvestre, Marc Sylvestre, Tom LaFary, Julia Krueger, Sean O'Toole, Stephen Rudie, Julie Schneider, Joe Schneider, Marty Gillaspy, Jenny Krueger, Mary Murray, Mike Murray, Mark Krueger (IN MEMORY OF), Jesse Abner, Dan Hawkins, Bill Getch, Vince Lombardi, Janie Lyons, Doug Lyons, Bob Krueger, Jim Krueger, Bill Krueger, Jim Conway, Roy Dale and the guys at the Findlay Street Gym, Bob York, Lisa Rimmer, Leigh Anne Stahl, Lisa Naimi, Moshe Naimi, AlisonSmith, Todd Smith, Greg Strowig, John L. York, Joan York, Kate Elsner, Karen Krubl, Kent Wellington, Joeliene Schaffer, Michael J. Magoto, Linda Kaminski, Anne York, Tom Bedacht, Guy York, Allison York, Julie York, Sheila Collins, Dick Zeinner, Anne McBreen, Bunny Jones, Menk Chatfield, John Merritt, Thomas Gilmore, Shannon Kennedy and to all those anonymous folks who sent their questionnaires back.

To Gina Bushman and Cyd Abner

Table of Contents

◆

Chapter 1: Boys Will Be Boys .... page 11
Chapter 2: Girl Things.. page 31
Chapter 3: Pickin' and Grinnin' .... page 41
Chapter 4: The Boob Tube .... page 49
Chapter 5: Driving Me Crazy .... page 57
Chapter 6: Food For Thought............................ page 67
Chapter 7: The Dating Game .... page 81
Chapter 8: The Wild Thing .... page 89
Chapter 9: The Potty .... page 99
Chapter 10: To Groom or Not To Groom .... page 109
Chapter 11: The Body Beautiful .... page 117

Chapter 12: Home Sweet Home .... page 123
Chapter 13: Best Friends and Pest Friends .... page 143
Chapter 14: All in the Family .... page 151
Chapter 15: Can We Talk? .... page 159
Chapter 16: Can We Argue? .... page 169
Chapter 17: The Dress Code .... page 175
Chapter 18: Malls and Balls .... page 181
Chapter 19: Z-Z-Z-Z-Z .... page 189
Chapter 20: Ho-Ho-Ho .... page 195
Chapter 21: Romance 101 .... page 199
Chapter 22: The Right Stuff .... page 215

Chapter 1:
Boys Will Be Boys

◆

The French author Francoise Sagan once said, "I like men to behave like men - strong and childish." According to our responses, she got exactly what she wanted.

"My husband thinks all blue colors match."

◆

"My husband loves paper plates, plastic forks and knives —
anything he doesn't have to wash."

◆

"I realize this is a generalization, but men tell you what you want
to hear and do what they want to do!"

◆

"Men fear women bosses.
Men fear women. Period.
Men fear women's periods.
Men fear women not having periods."

"Men often have bad breath, don't brush their teeth, have body odor and are overweight."

"My boyfriend can't resist the urge to tease pets — his own and other people's (hissing at the cat, roughing up the dog, etc.)."

"My husband is always hot, opens all the windows and has ten fans on when it's 30 degrees outside."

"When men play sports, they always use secret handshakes and nicknames like *Moose*!"

"Every time I'm in a bad mood he blames it on my period."

❖

"My husband thinks the louder something is, the better it is.
This applies to cars, chain saws, lawn mowers and himself."

❖

"He loves to use old macho sayings like, 'A man's got to do what
a man's got to do!' "

❖

"I hate when we're watching a sad movie and he keeps asking,
'Are you crying?', right at the saddest part."

"Whenever something smells gross, he has to emphasize it: Smell my feet, they're so sweaty and gross!"

"When he's having trouble fixing something around the house, he hits the object he's trying to fix and breaks it even worse."

"Why do all men refuse to use umbrellas? My husband always says, 'Get ready, we're going to make a run for it.'"

"I got more attention from my old boyfriend the week after I broke up with him than the entire three years we dated."

◆

"When my boyfriend is paying a lot of attention to me, it's because he either wants something or has done something wrong."

◆

"Men are bigger wimps than women when they're sick."

◆

"When I tell my boyfriend something, he pretends he already knows, just to show it's impossible for me to know something he doesn't."

"Men hate disco or any touch
dancing unless they're drunk
or over 40."

"He will push an elevator button repeatedly, thinking he'll get there faster."

"The only time I can drag him to a wedding with me is if he knows there is going to be a good spread of food and free beer."

"Men talk like they're an authority on every subject. I always beat him at tennis, yet he thinks he knows so much more."

"He can bait a hook, catch a fish and gut it with his bare hands, but he can't bring himself to pick up the *Kotex* wrapper."

"Come home occasionally."

"He can be as late as he wants, but when I'm a few minutes late he gets totally mad."

"I hate when he invites people over without asking. I'll typically have a messy house and plans to color my hair that night."

"Hey guys, here's a hint: Next time you try to cover a fart with a cough, try doing them at the same time."

"I hate when my boyfriend sticks his hands down his pants like *Al Bundy* on *Married With Children*."

"Men kill food, burn food, eat food,
make love, poop, sleep, kill food again."

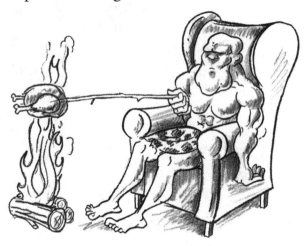

"My boyfriend once ate a live grasshopper for a six-pack of beer."

Chapter 2:
Girl Things

◆

Women - Creatures meant to be loved,
not to be understood.

- Oscar Wilde

"My wife is always cold. She keeps the heat high enough to cook a pot roast."

"Female gossip — No one is impervious from character assassination when two women get together to *talk.*"

"I always have to tell her we have to be somewhere an hour earlier than we're supposed to be there, and we're still late."

"Sometimes my wife has a dream about me cheating on her and when she wakes up she's mad at me."

"She snorts like a pig when she laughs. It's like being married to *Arnold Ziffel* on *Green Acres*."

"She analyzes my every utterance and how it might apply to her or our relationship."

"Women are picky, picky, picky."

"When a relationship ends, a woman will cry, get over it and get on with her life. On the other hand, it takes a man three years to get over it."

"My wife makes rules and changes them without warning."

"She is good at remembering names, birthdays and everything I've ever said."

◆

"My wife hints and expects me to read her mind."

◆

"My wife says things that make no sense like, 'Well, if you don't know what's wrong, I'm not going to tell you!'"

◆

"Women always cast a critical eye on other women when they enter a room."

"I hate the fact that if she breaks a nail it ruins her whole day."

"A woman will French kiss a man, but the thought of using his toothbrush is disgusting — Go figure."

❖

"If a woman ever tells you that it's okay to do something with the boys instead of going out with her — DON'T. It is NEVER okay."

❖

"My girlfriend is a tear factory. She can be watching a *Hallmark* commercial and start to cry."

❖

"Why do girls deny farts? You can be the only two people in the room and she will still deny it."

"Ever notice that women get starry-eyed at Mel Gibson's bare butt in a movie, but it's disgusting if the woman in the movie shows hers?"

"She shouldn't say, 'I don't care', when I ask her what she wants to do, only to later complain that she really would have liked to do something else."

"She has *rabbit ears* — hears everything within three blocks."

"My wife gets along with her friends but criticizes them behind their backs."

"My girlfriend remembers everything. She'll say, 'You were wearing a red flannel shirt, *Levi's 501* jeans and white deck shoes when you asked me out on our first date to see *Jaws 2.*' "

❖

"She always wants to know where I'm going, when I'm going, who I'm going with, who I'm going to see and why I'm going to see them. In other words — Nosy as Hell!"

Chapter 3:
Pickin' and Grinnin'

◆

The responses we received show that watching apes at the zoo incessantly picking, spitting, blowing and scratching is a good indication that Darwin's theory of evolution is probably correct.

"When my husband picks his nose, toes, bellybutton, eyes and any other orifice on his body, he never gets up to dispose of the pickings. I want to know where they go."

◆

"I think the only reason my husband grew a mustache was so he could constantly pick at it and bite it."

◆

"Men blow their noses by pressing one nostril with a finger and letting it fly."

◆

"I think it is totally gross when he pops his zits and leaves them on the bathroom mirror."

"Men pick their noses when they drive. It's like, the key goes in the ignition, the finger goes up the nose."

"He will sniff, and sniff, and SNNNIIFFFF for hours before breaking down and getting a tissue."

"My wife sprays some kind of spit out of her mouth when she yawns."

"I hate when my boyfriend uses chewing tobacco and leaves his gross spit cups all around the house."

"I think it's disgusting when men blow their nose in a handkerchief and then put it back in their pocket."

"I can't stand his constant nail biting. He gnaws until I think he won't have any fingers left."

"My wife uses her spit to clean spots off my shirt."

◆

"My boyfriend never gets rid of those gross *eye boogers* after he wakes up."

◆

"I hate when my boyfriend hockers in the kitchen sink."

◆

"Why do men scratch their crotch?"

◆

"She is constantly picking fuzz, string, hair and dirt from my clothes and face. I wish she would leave me alone."

"I hate when my husband sneezes and doesn't cover his mouth."

Chapter 4:
The Boob Tube

◆

Don't touch that dial! You'd think watching TV would be a simple activity that couldn't possibly annoy anyone. Wrong! Stay tuned for more comments on this topic.

"There will never be too many TV stations for my husband.
We have a satellite dish and he gets pleasure from watching
Bonanza in Japanese."

"He watches TV on the floor and gets a couch cushion for a pillow, but never puts it back on the couch when he goes to bed."

◆

"She watches silly shows like *Knots Landing* when classic reruns such as *The Andy Griffith Show* are on."

◆

"Remote control devices should never have been invented. I think I'm watching something and then BANG! Next thing I know, something else is on."

◆

"My husband battles with our kids over which cartoons they'll watch on Saturday mornings."

"I wish my wife would let me watch *Monday Night Football* in peace."

"When he is watching TV, I have to yell his name at least three times before he answers me."

"Before we got our remote control, I would be cleaning at one end of the house while he was firmly planted on the couch watching TV. He'd call for me, and when I got there, he'd ask me to change the channel."

"He can never just sit and watch a movie. He wiggles, makes weird noises and asks questions like, 'What are they going to do?' "

"Like moths to a flame, men are uncontrollably attracted to TV's in any environment. They can't stop themselves from watching, no matter what is on!"

"The only exercise my husband gets is through power changing the TV. The remote is inserted into his hand and he controls the channels viewed with a swift finger action."

❖

"He flips on the *Playboy Channel* when I leave the room, then flips it off when I return, thinking I didn't notice."

Chapter 5:
Driving Me Crazy

◆

Men view a car as an extension of their bodies and think driving laws are merely guidelines, while women believe putting oil in the car is messy and therefore optional. If you think these are the only differences, read on.

"I get a little nervous when my husband smokes a cigarette when filling the gas tank."

"Even though my husband knows absolutely nothing about cars, he always opens the hood as if through divine intervention he is going to solve the problem."

"He automatically assumes that if no one is around, it is his decision whether or not to stop at the stop sign or traffic light."

"It seems like every time I'm driving and I look over and see a woman driving by herself, she is singing along with the radio."

"He never washes the cars because he says the dirt and salt protect the paint - SURE! "

"When a man buys a car or works on a car, it is like a magnet.
Men come from all over the neighborhood to *check it out.*"

"My boyfriend gets in the car on his side and uses the automatic door lock instead of opening the door for me."

"I hate when he constantly switches the radio station in the car when we're driving."

"My husband always has to be the one to drive when we're in the car."

"With her as a passenger and me driving, every time something moves on the road I hear, 'watch that', 'stop', 'don't go so fast' . . ."

"My boyfriend never admits we're lost after taking one of his short cuts. He'll drive around for hours before asking for directions."

"Men say women can't drive; well, my husband can't drive a lick. If his head turns, the wheel turns."

◆

"She cries to me that something is wrong with her car - like I'm Mr. Goodwrench."

◆

"My wife always directs me around parking lots as if I'm driving with my eyes closed."

◆

"My girlfriend, for some unknown reason, going 65 MPH on the expressway, hits the brakes."

"My girlfriend always puts lipstick on when I'm driving, so I quickly hit the brakes to try to get her to mess up."

"My wife is like most women when it comes to cars. The car could be making all kinds of noises, and rather than getting it fixed or telling me, she merely turns up the volume on the radio."

"I wish she would move the car seat back to it's original position after she uses my car."

◆

"My husband always thinks he's in the right when he's driving. He'll cut everyone off, then he can't understand the ire of the other drivers when they honk and scream at him."

Chapter 6:
Food For Thought

◆

Whether we *eat to live* or *live to eat* doesn't matter. However, the *way* we eat does matter. At least it matters to a whole lot of men and women who responded to us. Here are some juicy tidbits for you to digest.

"I think women use *casserole* as a catch-all phrase for any kind of garbage which is left over that can be cooked in a crust with potato chips crunched on top."

"It really gets on my nerves when my husband crunches every single piece of ice in his glass."

"My husband drinks out of containers in the refrigerator instead of pouring a glass."

"I can always tell what my husband has eaten while I'm away from the house. A trail of crumbs follows him wherever he goes."

"It drives me crazy when my husband makes toast and butters it on the counter. Crumbs fly everywhere."

"My husband lays dirty spoons on the counter *next* to the spoon holder when he's cooking."

◆

"I hate when we're having dinner with guests and he says to one of them, 'Can I have a bite of your pie?' When they say yes, he takes out his teeth and slaps them in their pie."

◆

"My husband orders so much at fast food restaurants that he buys two drinks so the cashier doesn't think he is going to eat all the food himself."

◆

"I hate when we're at a restaurant and he wads the straw wrapper or paper napkin into little balls and tries to throw them in my drink."

"We can never agree on where to eat. He always wants to go to the *all-you-can-eat* pig-out joints, while I prefer romantic restaurants."

"When we go out to dinner with couples, the men's eating areas look as if the *Tasmanian Devil* ate there. As fat as my husband is, I don't know how he misses his mouth so much."

"My husband blames me when he farts. He says my cooking gives him gas."

"I don't like when my boyfriend just sits there and stares at me while I'm trying to finish my dinner."

"He'll put ketchup on anything. It insults my cooking. He has even put it on cottage cheese before."

"After dinner, he lets the dog eat off of my dishes!"

❖

"My husband will eat something after he drops it on the floor."

❖

"There is nothing like her mother's cooking. Whatever happened to 'Like mother like daughter'? My wife's famous for those surprise dinners like meat loaf-tater tot casserole or burnt beef stew guaranteed to clog your drain pipes."

❖

"My wife eats a lot more when she is cooking than she would have me believe."

"My husband concentrates on his food rather than making conversation."

◆

"My boyfriend doesn't think a pound of chocolate is more fattening than a pound of lettuce. He says, 'Eat a pound of anything and you will gain a pound.' "

◆

"I hate when she orders an expensive meal in a restaurant and only eats two bites."

◆

"When I make a cake or brownies, he cuts all his pieces out of the middle and leaves the outside edges for everyone else."

"My husband says, 'Are you gonna eat dat?', then steals it off my plate."

"He smacks his lips like a cow when he's chewing his food."

◆

"My husband sucks his teeth instead of flossing after meals. It's repulsive and the noise is irritating."

◆

"My husband is so gross when he eats. He takes all of the food on his plate and mixes it up into a pile of gunk and then eats it."

◆

"I wish she craved sex as much as she craves chocolate sundaes."

◆

"Like the King, he leaves his plate on the table, doesn't push in his chair and plops on the couch."

"My husband actually went through the drive-thru at *McDonald's* on the way to the hospital when I was in labor with our first child."

"My husband will eat cold pork and beans right out of the can. I think that is disgusting."

"I hate it when guys take a bite of their food, and while still chewing, take a big drink. I mean, what could that taste like?"

"Men eat too fast! They finish their dinner and they're ready to go, so women have to shovel their food in to keep up."

"My husband ends up with half the meal lodged in his teeth, and then proceeds to use anything from a credit card to his wedding ring to try to get it out."

"When I take my girlfriend to a fancy restaurant, I never get enough to eat. I usually stop at *White Castle* on the way home to get filled up."

Chapter 7:
The Dating Game

◆

The passion, the excitement, the risk, the sex, the fun, the disappointment, the rage, the jealousy, the rules...What rules? The people we questioned are still scratching their heads over this one.

"Although I hate to admit it, there are a lot of us women attracted to men who treat us like crap."

"Why do guys say they're going to do something with no intention of doing it? If you say you're going to call, then call!"

❖

"It bothers me that every time I get ready to go out, she tells me not to flirt with anyone. Why can't she trust me? I have only cheated on her once in the last nine months."

❖

"I hate that he seems to know every girl we pass by and he just has to stop and say 'Hi' to everyone of them."

❖

"I hate it when you are dating and there is no commitment and the dude gets jealous when you go out with someone else. But it's okay for him to do it."

"Some men have an attitude like 'take a number' if you want to schedule time with them. 'I'll see if I can work it in.'"

"Instead of telling you to get lost, women sometimes give out the wrong phone numbers."

$\blacklozenge$

"I really appreciate when my girlfriend offers to pay when we're on a date. Although I usually pay anyway, it lets me know she doesn't take it for granted."

$\blacklozenge$

"Guys ask you to do something then don't follow through. He'll say, 'This weekend we'll go to a concert in the park and grab a bite to eat.' I spend the rest of the week listening for weather reports, deciding what to wear, thinking about where to eat or maybe preparing a picnic. Meanwhile, he has completely forgotten his suggestion and calls at 5 o'clock to ask, 'What do you want to do tonight?' "

"Women think getting a man is like buying a house. They look for a fixer-upper, so they can convert him into what they want."

"When dating, why do guys always have to find out what their friends are doing before asking out their girlfriends?"

❖

"I hate when you are friends with a guy and when you suggest dating he says, 'I don't want to lose your friendship. It's too important to risk.' "

❖

"My ex-boyfriend constantly had to be the life of the party, and naturally I was always the butt of his hilarious jokes."

❖

"Why do guys tell girls they need *space* when they really want to see someone else?"

"When I'm out at a bar, I wish men would take more initiative and talk to me when it's obvious they like me. Instead, they just stare."

Chapter 8:
The Wild Thing

◆

Sex - The thing that takes up the least amount of time and causes the most amount of trouble.

- John Barrymore

"He still talks dirty to me after all these years of marriage."

◆

"I'd like to have sex without an appointment."

◆

"He washes himself off two seconds after having sex. I hate that."

◆

"On Valentine's Day I was sent handcuffs and a bottle of whipped cream."

◆

"I think it's great that she cleans me up after sex, but I nearly jump out of my skin when she uses a cold rag."

"Although it's the loving, caring thing to do, I hate having to snuggle after enjoying good sex. This is because I usually have to urinate with intense fury. After that, I'm more than happy to cuddle."

"I hate the *wet side* on my side of the bed."

◆

"I love when my wife prepares a brunch on a Sunday followed by a nude dip in the *Jacuzzi* and frolic on the grass, under the beautiful morning sun."

◆

"I wish he would last longer!"

◆

"High heels and a short teddy always look good before bedtime, or anytime!"

"My mate could be more creative in bed. She likes to do things I do, but sometimes I like to break out the whipped cream."

"I wish my husband would become impotent for a week."

◆

"Every so often when he comes over, I answer the door naked. Keeps him on his toes."

◆

"We make love and my husband says, 'Well, good night', and is snoring in two minutes."

◆

"When I'm at the sink with my hands in the dishwater, he's got his hands up my blouse and Grandma's in the next room!"

"When my wife wants to drive me crazy, she casually mentions at a restaurant that she is not wearing any underwear."

"One of those nights after staying up late with me and a screaming baby, he carried me into our study with an afghan, some amaretto and a favorite tape. We enjoyed a romantic interlude on the floor."

◆

"For my birthday, on one of the first times we were out alone since the baby was born, we went out for a romantic dinner then drove to my husband's office to make love."

◆

"Sometimes on Friday nights we play strip poker until we're naked and make love on the living room floor."

◆

"He could spend a little more time on foreplay."

"I'm 68 years old and my 70 year-old husband is a sex machine. He's still a horny little devil after all these years, and I love it."

"Whenever I'm really tired from a hard day at work, she takes me into the bedroom, removes my clothes, puts me on the bed and massages my entire body with warm lotion."

◆

"Have sex with me when I'm awake!"

◆

"I last longer in sex when I think of the *Flintstones*' theme song."

Chapter 9:
The Potty

◆

His and Hers, Ladies and Gentlemen, Guys and Gals, Boys and Girls, 🚹 and 🚺, call it what you want, but people told us that you'd better have two bathrooms if you expect to have harmony at home.

"He blows his nose in the shower. I hear him go *honnnnk* and wonder where that snot is going. I've got to clean that tub!"

"I wish he would pull all the little hairs off of the soap after he showers!"

"Why do women go to the john in groups?"

"I cannot stand when my boyfriend goes to the bathroom and doesn't wash his hands. Sometimes he will eat or even try to touch me after this - GROSS!"

"My wife has the illusion that her poop doesn't stink. Although sometimes her little trip to the powder room could bring tears to the eyes of Rocky Marciano."

"Why do men take newspapers or magazines into the bathroom? You get in and get out!"

"My husband pees in the shower instead of using the toilet which is two feet away."

❖

"I'm amazed that most women aren't bald. Just look at the bathroom sink when they're finished. Talk about hairballs!"

❖

"Why can't women put a new roll of toilet paper on after they use the last of it? I usually don't notice this until I need it, and then I have to walk to the closet with my pants around my ankles."

❖

"My husband always has to let me know he is going to relieve himself!"

"He leaves the bathroom smelling like the *Union Carbide* factory in Bhopal."

"I hate it when my boyfriend goes to the bathroom and dribbles pee down the front of the toilet onto the floor, where it leaves a sticky yellow stain."

"After showering, he'll drip dry all over the bathroom rug. Then I walk in to brush my teeth and my socks get soaked."

"I hate when he leaves the steamy shower door open while I'm trying to fix my hair."

"I hate when he goes to the bathroom and doesn't flush."

"I hate when my husband shaves and leaves little hairs all over the sink, all over the soap and sometimes even in my toothbrush."

"When a woman goes to the john, she turns the fan on, runs water, and makes all kinds of noise to drown out the sound of her going to the bathroom."

"He blows his nose on my clean bath towels and puts them back in the middle of the stack."

"Find a better place than the bathroom to hang your pantyhose or other delicate items. We don't hang our underwear in there."

"I wish she would put the damn cap back on the toothpaste."

"I hate it when he doesn't put the toilet seat down when he goes to the bathroom. I always end up falling in!"

Chapter 10:
To Groom or Not To Groom

❖

The reason we called this chapter To Groom or Not To Groom is because women *do* and men *don't*.

"Some men who are going bald comb that thin strand of hair from one side of their heads to the other. Who do they think they're kidding?"

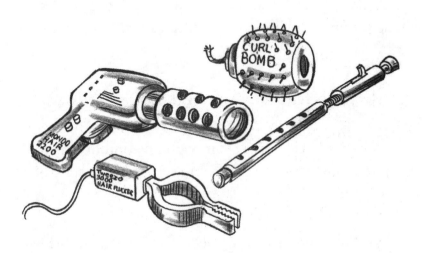

"My wife has an arsenal of gadgets that look more like weapons than personal grooming items."

"I can't understand why she says all she needs to do is put her makeup on (as if it will only be a minute), and it ends up seeming like an eternity."

❖

"I hate when guys have grease under their fingernails."

❖

"She has about 16 brands of shampoo and conditioners in the shower, each costing about $20. I have one big generic bottle which lasts all year."

❖

"I've resigned myself to one thing: My wife will never like her hair."

❖

"I always find my razor has taken the shape of a hacksaw blade after she has used it."

"My wife always wants to *style* my hair into some contemporary Don Johnson type look. I prefer barber shop cuts."

"He always misses a spot shaving and then rubs that particular spot all over my face until I feel like I've been sandblasted."

"The little hairs that grow out of
his ears and nose drive me nuts."

"I think my wife needs a putty knife to put all her makeup on. She wears way too much!"

Chapter 11:
The Body Beautiful

◆

Either it's too big, too small, too hairy, too wide, too thin, too short, too tall or too embarrassing to talk about. Here are some comments from those who *did* talk about it.

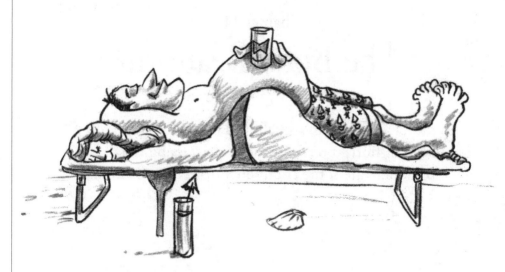

"Men get fat guts, women get fat butts."

"My husband avoids doctors because he thinks he is invincible."

"I hate when my wife is undressing and says, 'I'm going on a diet tomorrow.' "

"My wife says, 'Honey, you're not fat, you're just big-boned.' YEAH, RIGHT! My friends say I'm fat."

"We've spent tons of money on my wife's diet plans and she hasn't lost a pound. I cut out sweets and started running two miles a day and have lost almost 20 pounds."

"My husband thinks it's okay for him to be flabby or out of shape, but I'm supposed to look like a fashion model."

❖

"My girlfriend always thinks she needs to lose weight, no matter how thin she is."

❖

"When I cut myself, I wash it, apply antiseptic and a *Band-Aid*. When my husband cuts himself he does nothing. Two days later, when the *boo-boo* is infected, I have to play nursemaid and assure him it won't be amputated."

❖

"She could use some major help from the *boob fairy*."

"My boyfriend should consider shaving some of the hair off his back."

Chapter 12:
Home Sweet Home

◆

Since the first caveman rolled a rock in front of a cave and called it home, men and women have been at odds on how to run a household. It's either a case of someone doing too much - or not enough. So sit back, kick your shoes off and see what our respondents had to say on this matter.

"My husband's name is *One Trip Bob*. We have to bring all the groceries into the house in one trip. He'll say, 'Put a bag under my arm, on my head, between my legs...' "

"My wife acts as if cleaning the bathroom can possibly be as hard as cleaning gutters, mowing the grass or shoveling snow."

◆

"I hate when he leaves used *Q-tips* and toenail clippings on the nightstand."

◆

"My husband rams into every piece of nice furniture we have when he is vacuuming. He says he needs to get real close to get all the dirt."

◆

"Somehow the marriage vows must have taken the *neat cells* out of my husband, because now he seems to drop his underwear approximately ten inches from the hamper."

"I know my husband pees in our pool, but he won't admit it. He stands in the pool with a little grin on his face as he relieves himself."

"My husband turns on the gas grill and waits a few minutes to light the match. He then acts surprised when he lights the grill and a small explosion occurs."

"The ice cube tray must be a very complicated device because it never seems to get refilled in our house"

◆

"I can't tell you how many clothes my wife has ruined in the wash. The reds fade into whites and clothes that once fit have shrunk. It seems like everything I wear is pink and too small."

◆

"My husband pees in the backyard in broad daylight when he is cutting the grass."

◆

"What matters to her is not that I help, but that I offer to help. Because whenever I try to help, she says I'm no help and could I please go watch TV and stay out of her way."

"My husband has a favorite chair that's exclusively his. No one else dares to sit in it."

"My husband would like the vacuum cleaner to be strong enough to pick anything out of the carpet, including gum and glue."

"When you're working with a tool trying to put something together and you, a woman, ask for advice, the man pulls the tool out of your hand and says, 'Here, let me do it.'"

"I will never understand why she insists we make our bed everyday."

"I dust under things, my husband dusts around things. His logic: How could dust get under anything?"

"Every time we're ready to walk out the door, she finds something else to do inside."

"Why can't men understand the mechanics of operating a washing machine? I guess pulling out that big knob is kind of tricky."

"His *do-it-yourself* projects cost us twice as much as hiring the right people or buying the right things in the first place."

"How can men tune out everything happening around them?
He can be reading and the kids are coloring on the wall in the
same room and he doesn't see it."

"The only things my husband takes care of are his tools. If I go to open a paint can, my husband tells me NOT to use the *Craftsman* screwdriver! Oh, excuse me!"

◆

"My husband will make a mess, and when I clean it up, he complains because he can't find anything."

◆

"I hate having to wash brown stains from his underwear."

◆

"My husband rarely disposes of his beer cans and bottles. He lines them up on the kitchen table as if they are trophies."

◆

"I hate when my husband tracks mud in the house. He denies it, even though the footprints are of his size 12 wing tips."

"I hate when he works out, comes in the house all sweaty and then sits on the furniture before taking a shower!"

"When my husband cuts
the grass, he cuts flowers,
poles, sewer lids, small
varmints and the kids'
toys."

"Dishes make it into the sink but never the dishwasher. Is the door too heavy for him to pull down?"

◆

"She always says things like, 'Don't burn yourself', 'Be careful', 'Don't cut yourself', as if I'm deliberately trying to hurt myself."

◆

"My wife enjoys maintaining plants throughout the home. When watering the plants, she also waters the tables and the rugs."

◆

"When a man does something unexpected like cleaning the kitchen or dusting, he is just like a puppy who runs back to you for praise. He needs to be told, 'What a good boy!' "

"He thinks things get cleaned by magic. Plates and cups walk into the kitchen after games on TV."

"I think he holds the belief that dirt is our friend."

"My husband plays dumb to get out of doing household chores."

◆

"I hate when he does the laundry. He launders bath towels, dirty rags and my underwear all together."

◆

"I hate when he reads the Sunday paper and doesn't let me pull the Fashion section out because it messes up his neat pile."

◆

"My wife is so picky about putting groceries in the right place. Heaven forbid if I put the bean soup next to the tuna fish!"

"He doesn't put lids on containers tight enough, so when they're picked up the lids come off and stuff goes everywhere."

" I hate when my husband farts around the house, especially in front of the children. He then wonders where they pick up their bad habits."

Chapter 13:
Best Friends and Pest Friends

◆

Friends - those pesky little diversions that take up all of your mate's time, undermine your relationship, throw up on your couch and ultimately end up being in YOUR wedding.

"I knew my best friend was in love when he started accessorizing his clothes. His belts started matching his socks. It was a sad day."

"It seems like when we go to parties, all the guys are in the living room watching sports and all the girls are in the kitchen gossiping."

❖

"He and his friend are like *Ralph Kramden* and *Ed Norton*. They always seem to have some get-rich-quick scheme that has them occupied for days or months."

❖

"I hate when my boyfriend treats me real nice when we're alone and like dog meat when we're with his friends."

"It seems my boyfriend only parties and gets crazy when he's out with his friends on Friday. Then we always stay home for a quiet evening on Saturday. Why can't *we* go out and get crazy?"

"My girlfriend is too concerned about hurting her friends' feelings. She beats around the bush instead of saying, 'No, I don't want to do that.'"

◆

"When her friends come over it seems to take them as long to say their goodbyes as the length of the entire visit. Just say goodbye and go!"

◆

"My husband is so gullible. With a six-pack of beer and some pizza he can be bribed to work at a friend's house all day. Why can't I get him to work around our house?"

"He and his friends fart, cuss, burp, snort and spit as if they are in a contest."

"Whenever he says he's going to have a *few beers* with his friends, it ends up being a *few cases*."

"She hates when I go to a friend's bachelor party, but from what I hear, her bachelorette parties make us look like cub scouts."

"My husband expects me to be good friends with his friends' wives, but makes no effort to be friends with my girlfriends' husbands."

"My girlfriend hangs out with guys who she says just want to be friends. But I know better."

Chapter 14:

All in the Family

They're creepy and they're kooky, mysterious and spooky;
They're altogether ooky, the quotes on family.

"It makes me sick when his parents treat him like a little boy!
He's 50 and still acts like a child."

"When our first son was born, he was baptized on Super Bowl Sunday and none of my husband's family showed up."

❖

"I hate the fact that we have to go to all of her family's events, including her third cousin's birthday party."

❖

"His brother walks in our house without knocking, eats everything in the refrigerator and sits down to watch TV without saying a word."

"The best thing about my girlfriend's dad is he has every copy of *Playboy Magazine* ever published."

"I hate going to her parents' house in the middle of a family argument and they ask me who I think is right. It really puts me on the spot."

❖

"It bothers me when my husband says the children look like him all the time and never anything about me."

❖

"My mother-in-law always tries to get me to cook the same meals for my husband that she did, when I'm a better cook in the first place."

"I very much dislike her mother!"

"I hate going to his house because his dad always has to show me all the trophies and awards the family has ever won."

"I dread eating at her parents' house because they all eat like birds and I can't eat as much as I want without feeling like a pig."

◆

"Every time we have a fight, she tells her mom *her* side of the story so I sound like the bad guy."

◆

"When I'm trying to fix something at my house, her dad always comes over and tries to show me a better way to do it."

Chapter 15:
Can We Talk?

◆

Did you ever try to talk to your mate and BLAH, BLAH, BLAH, BLAH, BLAH, BLAH... BLAH... BLAH... BLAH, BLAH...Well, our responses indicate the key to good communication is BLAH, BLAH, BLAH, BLAH, BLAH, BLAH... BLAH... BLAH... BLAH, BLAH . . . Are you listening to us?

"My favorite saying is, 'Yes dear, yes dear.' "

"He's hard of hearing at the most opportune times."

"I hate when your wife thinks she knows you so well that she tries to finish your sentences for you."

"I come home tired and hungry at 10 p.m. and she has something to tell me. I listen for half an hour and she still isn't getting to the point. When I ask, 'What's the point?', she blows up saying, 'You never listen to me!' "

"I hate when I'm on the phone with my mate and he burps in my ear."

"Sometimes on a long drive with my wife I have to say, 'Can we be quiet now?', because I'm done talking."

◆

"I hate when I ask him a question and he doesn't answer, so I have to keep repeating the question!"

◆

"I don't particularly like when I'm trying to express a deep feeling and this ridiculous grin appears on her face as if she's mocking me."

◆

"I hate when women answer a question with a question like, 'When did I have time to go to the cleaners?' "

"My wife always wants to have serious discussions at midnight
when I need to get up early and want to sleep."

"Ask my wife what time it is and she'll tell you how to build a watch."

"Famous last words from my wife: 'Just be honest with me, I won't get mad.' Yeah, right!"

"My wife shouldn't say, 'It's nothing', when I ask her what's wrong."

"Women should get egg timers when talking so they'll know when they're done."

"I wish I could figure a way to hook the mute button on the remote control up to my wife so I could enjoy a little peace and quiet."

"He respects my opinion even if we disagree."

❖

"She says, 'I love you', and waits for my response. I hate that!"

❖

"She talks out of the blue about the most irrelevant subjects."

❖

"I hate when my girlfriend calls me on the phone and doesn't say anything."

❖

"I hate when she asks me, 'What are you thinking?' "

"I hate when I'm talking to my boyfriend on the phone and he acts like he is listening and keeps saying, 'Uh huh, uh huh.' I know he is watching TV, but he won't admit it."

"Is it too much to ask for my husband to have an occasional conversation with me after dinner instead of heading directly for the couch?"

◆

"Women just *have* to talk to you, even if you are obviously in the middle of something important."

◆

"When I tell my wife something confidential you can bet she will tell the person I don't want to know."

◆

"I wish my girlfriend would say exactly what she feels instead of worrying that she will say the wrong thing and our relationship will end."

Chapter 16:
Can We Argue?

◆

This is the same as Chapter 15 - Only louder!

"He avoids arguments by just not responding. He thinks I will eventually wear myself out."

◆

"We have agreed to finish all fights before bedtime, never hang up on each other and never criticize each other in public. These are very important for any relationship."

◆

"Just one time in my life I would like to have a tape recording of one of our arguments. This way she couldn't blame me for things I don't remember saying in the first place."

◆

"He always has to have the last word."

"I despise when my girlfriend turns from a
   normal person into a big-eyed-let's-snuggle-
   dedicated-to-your-love gerbil whenever I'm
   really mad at her."

"I hate when he hits below the belt during an argument. He'll bring up things from the past like when I accidently ran over his dog."

"After an argument has been resolved, she keeps trying to make a point as to why she was correct and I was wrong."

"Women argue in a way that you can't win, and when you do, you still lose."

"My boyfriend tries to turn everything around and make me feel guilty when I'm mad at him, even when I had a good reason to be."

"I can't stand when my boyfriend thinks an argument will
be over with and forgotten if he
brings me flowers."

Chapter 17:
The Dress Code

◆

Based on our feedback, there is only one dress code: There is nothing too old for a man to wear and nothing new enough for a woman to wear. Two distinct perspectives for a species God probably wanted to be naked in the first place.

"My husband refuses to part with his old clothing."

"He is neat but dirty. All his clothes are folded and neatly tucked away, but half of them have been worn three or four times."

"My wife irons great, as long as you like three or four creases in each pant leg."

"He doesn't wear socks with his shoes and then wonders why his feet smell so bad."

"My wife says there are different colors of white that go with different outfits. I say, white is white."

"Why does my wife always say, 'You're not going to wear *that*, are you?'"

"Men can't put an outfit of clothing together. They need *Garanimals*."

"Sometimes on the weekends my husband doesn't wear underwear. He says *they* need to breathe after the work week. What if his zipper comes down in front of someone like my mom?"

◆

"My wife refuses to wear the same dress to two different weddings."

◆

"Men decide what they are going to wear when they get dressed. Women decide two weeks in advance."

◆

"My husband will wear good clothes to work in the yard or on the car, and then he wears rags when we go out together."

"My wife changes her clothes about nine times before finally deciding which outfit to wear."

Chapter 18:
Malls and Balls

◆

The crowds. The rush to get to the line. The mass of humanity defending their territory, and finally, the thrill of capturing the prize. It's easy to see how comments on sports and shopping ended up in the same chapter.

"My wife will buy anything if it's on sale, then tell me how much she saved."

❖

"My husband's memory is shrinking. I send him to the store for two items and he comes home with two different items because he couldn't remember what he went for."

❖

"We're broke until a golf game comes up."

❖

"My wife cannot understand that you can only spend so much money and still have enough left for those unimportant things like rent, food and car payments."

"I hate having to carry my girlfriend's purse while in a store. No matter how many different ways I try to carry it, it just doesn't feel manly!"

"When my husband watches sports, he slouches down in the *La-Z-Boy* and looks like a jellyfish holding a beer."

❖

"I wish my husband would say, 'I like the outfit you bought', instead of, 'How much?' "

❖

"My wife browses at the store with no plan of action on what is going to be purchased. I go to the store, buy what I need and leave."

❖

"Maybe this applies to all men: He always has to see what's on *ESPN* when we're watching TV."

"He doesn't like to shop so he thinks that excuses him from buying me presents."

◆

"My husband has a disorder called sportsaphelia. If he doesn't get his weekly fix of TV sports, *we* have a miserable week."

◆

"He should quit complaining about how I spend money: the cleaners, groceries, kids' baseball fee, ballet outfit, etc. . . . Like this is how I really want to spend it!"

◆

"Whenever he is with his friends, the topic of conversation is sports. He knows every detail about every player who ever lived, but he can't seem to remember my middle name."

"My husband always buys me gifts that he uses more than I do. Recently, he bought me a compact disc player which is now located in *his* den."

◆

"My husband flat out refuses to buy tampons for me at the store because it embarrasses him."

◆

"Even though our husbands act like they're sports gurus, it seems me and my girlfriends always win the betting pools by picking teams with the prettiest uniforms."

◆

"Shopping malls! They are all alike, yet women treat each visit to the mall like a once-in-a-lifetime fashion exhibition."

"There is nothing like a girlfriend telling you that you played just great in that last game, even though the balance of the universe knows you should have been denied a license to play sports in the first place."

"I hate when she buys me something I don't want. I can't tell her I don't like it, so I end up stuck with it!"

◆

"My wife has to examine every item of clothing in the store before she decides what to buy."

◆

"Electronics stores are filled with men who have been dragged to the mall to shop. They try to catch a glimpse of the game on TV."

◆

"Women are much more thoughtful in picking out gifts than men are. My husband once gave me a cheese basket for our anniversary."

Chapter 19:
Z-Z-Z-Z-Z

Flying elbows, snoring, sweating, drooling, shivering and that quick-kick-of-the-leg thing that has yet to be defined, all provide for an interesting and dangerous night between the sheets. Read on to see what other things people are losing sleep over.

"I dislike him assuming that every time we get ready for bed, it's his cue to start bugging me."

❖

"My wife drools when she sleeps."

❖

"My wife will not stay on her side of the bed when sleeping, keeping me up all night so I'm grouchy the next day."

❖

"She always wants to snuggle when I'm uncomfortably hot."

❖

"She steals all the covers at night."

"His snoring is sometimes so loud it scares me and wakes me up!"

"It seems my husband is quiet as a church mouse all night, and then when we get to bed, he farts. It's like he saves them just for me."

"He makes more noise trying not to wake me up than if he would turn the lights on and go about his business."

◆

"My husband thinks he needs more sleep than I do. I get up at 3 a.m. to attend to our crying baby. When I wake him up he yells at me because he has to get up early. So do I!"

Chapter 20:
Ho-Ho-Ho

Jingle bells, trees from hell, presents to take back;
Christmas lights, family fights and quotes on
Christmas crap.

"My husband is such a *Charlie Brown* at Christmas. Each year I send him out to get a tree. Each year he brings back a big ugly bush with no needles."

"I hate going to her parents' house at Christmas because they always make me join in these ridiculous Christmas sing-a-longs by the piano."

"Our house looks like Las Vegas at Christmas time. My husband insists on having Santa and half the North Pole lit up in our front yard."

"My wife just has to see all her friends and family at Christmas, so we spend half our time driving to the different parties and only get to stay a few minutes."

"Men Christmas shop at the last minute."

"His brother always gives our son these gross presents like *Slime* that mess up our whole house."

Chapter 21:

Romance 101

◆

Do sweet notes, roses, candlelit baths, Johnny
Mathis, surprise weekends and long, slow kisses
really work? . . . YEP!

"He is not too romantic but he has a heart of gold."

◆

"One cold winter night, my boyfriend called me and said, 'It's going to be real cold tonight and I would like to come over and keep you warm.' He came over with hot chocolate and marshmallows and we snuggled all night.

◆

"One of the things he said to me years ago was he'd make my fantasies come true. Every woman needs a man like that. We are both getting to that 40-something age and we still love to play at romance."

"Me and my boyfriend work in the same office building, and sometimes when we meet in the hallway, he plants a long, spontaneous kiss on me. It's kind of risky but I love it."

"I came home late from work one night to find that my wife had deliberately strewn clothing leading into the bedroom where she was waiting with a nice dinner, champagne and a negligee."

◆

"A guy in my office planned an awesome three-day weekend in San Francisco for his girlfriend. He arranged a day off with her boss, packed her clothes and picked her up after work. She had no idea what the deal was until they got to the airport."

◆

"Candlelit baths are the best. One night my fiance and I took a late night bath together and just laid in each others arms in the warm water with our eyes shut. It was total euphoria!"

"When we were in San Diego I saw a stuffed bear I liked. He said it was too expensive. Then later he had it shipped to me for Valentine's Day."

"We take summer weekend camping trips and sleep under the stars, take long hikes together and sit by a campfire in the evening."

◆

"On our first anniversary my husband and I watched our wedding video, looked at our pictures, smashed cake in each other's faces, danced to our song and then made love on our back deck."

◆

"A friend of mine sent a dozen roses to his bride on the morning of their wedding. What a great way to start the honeymoon."

"I find it very romantic if a man is a good ballroom-type dancer. If he can take the lead and twirl you around, dip you here and there, it is fun and makes you feel like a lady."

"When I least expect it, he buys me a piece of expensive jewelry and sends me on a treasure hunt to find it. It doubles the excitement!"

"I'd like to have flowers sent to me other than when I'm in the hospital giving birth or having an operation."

"On our first Valentine's Day as a married couple, my husband had roses delivered to the office with a key to a downtown hotel room. I met him there for a wonderfully romantic evening."

"We've been married too long for romance."

"The best way to enhance a relationship is to have a romantic evening of *Bud* in the bottle, pizza on the plate and a classic *Rambo* movie on the VCR."

"For me, the most romantic moment was in the delivery room right after our son was born. We hugged and cried. I think romance has a lot to do with love and this was definitely the most loving time of our lives!"

◆

"I love it when he gives me long, slow kisses."

◆

"Our 22 years of marriage have all been romantic! On our anniversary we go away to a hotel with a swimming pool and *Jacuzzi.* We don't come up for air until it is time to check out! A new nightie and a smile are all we need!"

"We took a bath together and had bath toys."

"It's hard to be humble when your wife is as beautiful as mine."

❖

"I like when we are out at a party, and when my husband catches a glimpse of me from across the room, he winks."

❖

"For my birthday, my husband planned a surprise night out for me and two of my closest girlfriends. He bought me a new outfit, rented a limo and prepaid our dinner. It was a wonderful *ladies'* night out.' "

❖

"Whenever my wife goes out of town for a couple of days, she leaves me numerous notes around the house reminding me of special times, or if nothing else, how much she loves me."

"My girlfriend and her husband went out for dinner on their tenth anniversary. While at dinner, she noticed a string on the edge of his suit pocket. Being a dutiful wife, she reached to pull the offending thread from his jacket. She pulled and pulled and the thread was five feet long! She was in shock and the people sitting close to them were staring. At the end of this long thread was tied a beautiful diamond ring, the ring he couldn't afford to buy her ten years earlier."

"I love when I'm at work and my boyfriend calls me out of the blue to tell me he's thinking of me. It's even better when he shows up to see me *just because.* "

◆

"Ro-what???"

◆

"On my birthday a few years ago he took me horseback riding. We went down a quiet trail and came upon a stand of trees. He stopped, got off his horse and pulled aside some bushes to reveal a bottle of champagne, balloons and some fruit and cheese he had hidden earlier. It was very romantic."

"I would appreciate flowers once in a while. My boyfriend is too practical. He'll say, 'What's the purpose of spending all that money when they die in two days?'"

◆

"I had a blind date years ago, and to my surprise I received flowers the Wednesday before the date. It turned out the flower delivery man *was* my date. I didn't realize this until he told me on the night we went out."

◆

"After a long day of running around at work in high heel shoes, I come home tired and irritable and my husband gives me the most wonderful foot massages. He knows how to put the smile back on my face."

Chapter 22:
The Right Stuff

◆

This is the day-in and day-out stuff that makes living with each other's faults a little easier. It'll never go out of style. So if you want to grow old together, these comments will lead the way.

"My wife is the first person in my life who believes in me more than even myself. She has made me realize my potential and inspires me to be a very good man."

◆

"He gives me special notes during those tough times."

◆

"When I talk to my husband about something that is very important to me such as a career change, he has a sincere interest and talks to me about it. I really like that."

◆

"My lady is very independent and takes pride in standing on her own two feet, but gentle enough to know she can lean on me when she needs to."

"After a bad day at work, my girlfriend will have a cold beer ready for me and then give me a back massage."

"My husband is really generous, often putting my needs before his own. If I really want something, like clothes or jewelry, he always finds a way to buy it for me even if money is tight at that time."

◆

"He's always affectionate. He hugs me, tells me I look good and that he loves me."

◆

"His patience balances out my lack of it."

◆

"My husband seems to have a sixth sense when it comes to my feelings. He knows just the right time to plan a special weekend at the beach or a night out at my favorite restaurant."

"He wipes my forehead with a wet cloth whenever I throw up!"

◆

"I like when he tells me I look good when I've gotten dressed up."

◆

"He's a gentleman. He opens doors, helps me with my coat and pushes my chair in."

◆

"The day my father died my boyfriend came to my house after he got off work. He sat in a rocking chair and held me while I rattled on and on about nothing."

◆

"I like when he calls me and tells me he misses me."

"I have a real weakness for animals and I find it very attractive when a guy has a soft spot for furry critters. It shows me he can care about something besides himself."

◆

"I try to buy him special treats when I go out."

◆

"I love when my husband spontaneously holds my hand and give me little hugs and kisses while we're watching TV, for no reason except that he loves me."

◆

"He always tells me, 'Thank you', 'I love you' and 'I'm so glad I've got you.'"

◆

"We really talk to each other. Really talk. Daily."

"My husband is my best friend."

Dear Reader,

If you have some humorous observations or unique insights on relationships that you care to share with us, please write them down with your name, age and address and mail them to us. We would welcome the opportunity of sharing them with other readers in a future book. Thank you!

◆

The Armchair Press
3616 White Oak Drive
Suite 2
Cincinnati, Ohio 45247

About the Authors

Brian Krueger has been President of Krueger Advertising for eight years. He is an avid illustrator and cartoonist, whose illustrations have appeared in *Playboy Magazine* and *Writer's Digest.* He considers himself an armchair expert on various topics, including his relationship with his girlfriend Cyd. He enjoys boxing, the Rolling Stones and is from a family of nine children. He currently resides in Cincinnati, Ohio.

Jack York is President of York Ventures, Inc. His passions include travel, Tennessee Volunteer football, country music, his family, and his girlfriend Gina. He is the self proclaimed *World's Cleanest Guy,* who promises to do most of the housework. He currently resides in Cincinnati, Ohio.